IS THERE LIFE IN THE ARCTIC TUNDRA?

SCIENCE BOOK AGE FOR KIDS 9-12

CHILDREN'S NATURE BOOKS

BABY PROFESSOR

EDUCATION KIDS

Speedy Publishing LLC

40 E. Main St. #1156

Newark, DE 19711

www.speedypublishing.com

Copyright 2017

In this book, we're going to talk about the Arctic tundra. So, let's get right to it!

WHAT IS A BIOME?

Rainforests, deserts, grasslands, and tundra may all seem very different from each other, but they are all biomes. A biome is a community of animals and plants in a specific type of climate. Biomes are composed of similar ecosystems. Ecosystems are communities of organisms that live and interact with each other within certain types of physical environments.

WHAT IS THE ARCTIC TUNDRA?

The Arctic tundra was formed about 10,000 years ago, so it's the youngest biome in the world. It is a harsh, cold, dry biome with ecosystems that are regions void of trees. Throughout the entire year, the climate is tremendously cold and very windy. There is very little rain. The lands are covered with snow for most of the year except for the summer season, which blossoms with fields of wildflowers.

Almost all regions of tundra are situated in the Northern Hemisphere at latitudes of 55 degrees to 70 degrees north. Most of the tundra on Earth surrounds the North Pole and covers about 1/5 of the Earth's surface.

There are small areas that are like tundras in Antarctica, which is in the Southern Hemisphere. However, it's actually colder there than in the Arctic, so the ground is constantly covered with snow or ice or both. Conditions there are not exactly right for a true tundra.

The word tundra comes from the word "tunturia" in the Finnish language. It translates to "barren ground." The ground in tundra biomes is always frozen under the surface. The depth of ground that's frozen is anywhere from as little as 10 inches deep to as much as 3 feet. Because of this permanently frozen ground called permafrost, tree roots can't grow, so there are no trees. Even though the ground is barren and rocky, some types of plants can still grow.

Permafrost

Mosses as well as lichen and heaths all grow low to the ground so they can live on the rocky, barren surfaces.

There are four seasons in the tundra. However, the spring season is very short in between the long winter and summer seasons. The same is true for fall, which is only a short separator between summer and winter.

Arctic Redpoll

The tundra has long winters that last about 8 months. The winter is very cold and there is very little sunlight so it's dark for much of the time even during the day. During the summertime, the topmost layer of the permafrost starts to melt. It makes the ground soggy so it transforms the tundra into marshes and bogs as well as lakes and streams. It becomes the perfect breeding ground for thousands of insects. Attracted by the insects they can eat, migratory birds stop there to fill up on food.

WHAT IS THE TEMPERATURE LIKE IN THE TUNDRA?

The tundra's average temperature year round is only -18 degrees Fahrenheit and in the winter it can go down to a temperature of -94 degrees Fahrenheit! During the winter months, nighttime lasts for weeks on end and the sun is barely visible due to the angle of the Earth. In the Arctic regions it's essentially night for half the year and day for the other half of the year.

The tundra in North America and those in Scandinavia and Russia differ in temperature. The tundra in Scandinavia is warmer than the other two with a winter temperature average of 18 degrees Fahrenheit.

During the summer, the opposite is true than the darkness of the winter months. The summer months have sun virtually 24 hours every day. That is why the Arctic regions have been described as "The Land of the Midnight Sun." Summer is much warmer than winter, although it wouldn't be considered warm in other areas of the Earth. The temperature has been known to get up to 54 degrees Fahrenheit, but it can get as cold as 37 degrees Fahrenheit even during the summer.

As if the cold wasn't harsh enough, the wind in the Arctic tundra is punishing as well. The wind blows from 30 to 60 miles per hour on most days.

HOW MUCH RAIN DOES THE TUNDRA GET?

When it comes to rain, the tundra is similar to a cold desert. As little as 6 inches and as many as 10 inches of precipitation fall each year and it is primarily in the form of snow. Because of the permafrost, the ground stays frozen all through the year. During the summer, the top layer thaws enough for liquid water to remain on the surface.

It's not enough for the deeper layers to defrost, so the water can't absorb into the ground. That's why the melting snow and frost forms lakes and other watery areas so quickly. The water on the surface has nowhere to go. There's just enough liquid water for plants to grow and quickly reproduce.

WHAT TYPES OF PLANTS GROW IN THE TUNDRA?

It's amazing that anything lives in the harsh environment of the tundra, but actually over 1,500 species of plants live there. There are no trees due to the permafrost, with the exception of a few types of birch trees in the warmer latitudes. However, there are all types of ground cover including shrubs, lichens, mosses, and grasses.

Saxifrage

Willows grow there as well, although they usually don't get more than 3 inches in height. There are also about 400 different types of flowering plants. A few examples of plants that live there are artic moss, bearberry, caribou moss, arctic willow, labrador tea, diamond-leaf willow, tufted saxifrage, and pasque flower. Many plants have furry or waxy coatings to protect them from the cold and wind.

The growing season is about two months long so the plants must grow and reproduce fast. Many of these plants have a dense layer of roots, which have been established over centuries of growth. The soil doesn't have many nutrients except for animal wastes that act as fertilizers. Some of the plants that grow in the tundra can actually grow underwater, which gives them an advantage when there are temporary lakes on the surface of the tundra.

Bearberry

Arctic Wolf

WHAT TYPES OF ANIMALS LIVE IN THE TUNDRA?

The animals that live in the tundra have adapted to survive in the harsh environment. Although there are not many types of animals that live there, the over 40 species of mammals that do sometimes reach large numbers in terms of population. For example, in the North American tundra, large herds of caribou graze on the ground-cover plants. These caribou are known as reindeer in Europe.

Musk-oxen travel in herds too, although the herds are smaller than the caribou herds. Deer in herds and the more solitary moose can be found there as well.

Musk-Ox

Arctic Fox

There are also mammals that are predators. Polar bears, arctic foxes, wolves, and wolverines are all carnivores and hunt other animals to survive. Smaller mammals, such as snowshoe rabbits, wild hares, rodents of different types, lemmings, and shrews also live in the tundra and are food for the predators.

Birds

During the months when the tundra is marshy, migratory birds come in the thousands. The harlequin duck with its unique black and white stripes migrates there. Different types of sandpipers as well as plovers are common during the summer season.

Harlequin Duck

Snowy Owl

Ptarmigans and snowy owls are year-round residents of the tundra. The ptarmigans are brown in the summer and white in the winter to blend into the environment. With its white feathers, the snowy owl can barely be seen in the white snow.

Insects

The thousands of insects during the summer months can make it difficult for people to be outdoors. Flies, such as black flies and deer flies, breed in great numbers.

Black Fly

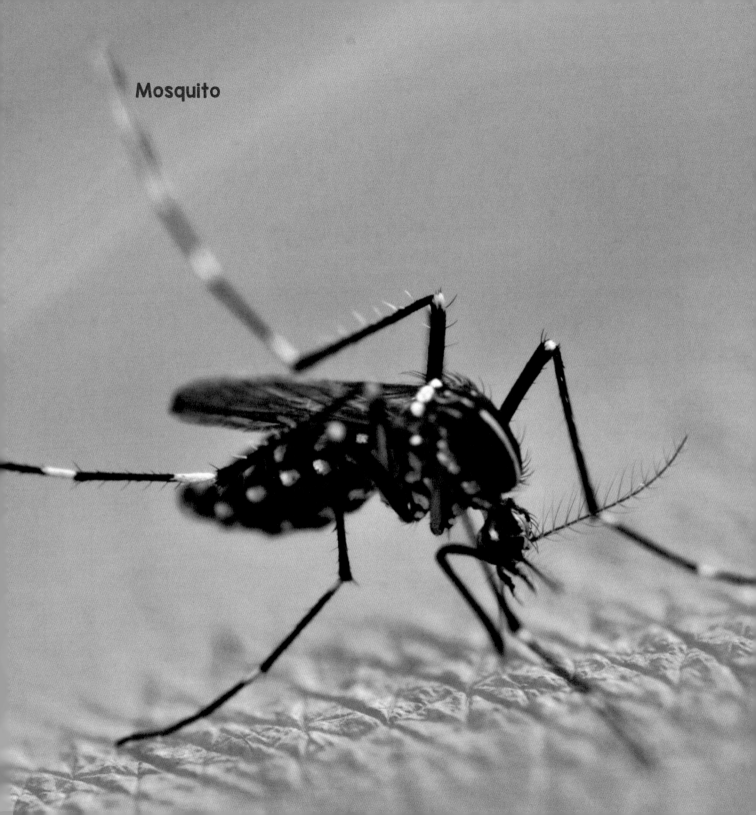

Mosquito

Mosquitoes and small biting midges, nicknamed "no-see-ums" because of their small size, are a constant nuisance. Mosquitoes survive the winter months because they have a way to replace their body water with glycerol, which acts just like an antifreeze so their bodies don't freeze.

They can survive under snow banks during the winter due to this special antifreeze. Tundra bumblebees have thick hair that protects their bodies from getting too cold.

Bumblebee

THE CARBON DIOXIDE BALANCE

The Arctic tundra is critical to the balance of carbon dioxide in the atmosphere. During the shorter summer months, the plants that live in the tundra take in carbon dioxide. Under normal conditions, these plants would eventually die and decompose giving off carbon dioxide. However, since the time period is so short and the temperatures are so cold, the plants don't decompose. The result is that the Arctic tundra takes in more carbon dioxide than it gives off.

WHY IS THE TUNDRA A FRAGILE ENVIRONMENT?

Because the tundra is so harsh in terms of its climate, the environment is very fragile. When there are environmental changes, they often have disastrous consequences. For example, when traditional feeding grounds of polar bears are disrupted by oil pipelines, oil rigs, or mining activities, many of the animals starve to death.

Polar Bear

THERE IS LIFE IN THE ARCTIC TUNDRA!

Despite its harsh, cold, windy environment, the Arctic tundra is a critical biome. Many plants and animals have adapted to the conditions and have survived during the long, dark, freezing winters and the short, insect-ridden summers. However, it's a fragile environment that needs protection. Small stresses can bring quick destruction to the communities of organisms that live there.

Now that you've learned about the animals and plants of the Arctic tundra, you may want to read about two other places that have unique flora and fauna in the Baby Professor book Australia and Oceania: The Smallest Continent, Unique Animal Life.

Made in the USA
Middletown, DE
28 February 2022

61943958R00038